ARPEGGIOS FOR GUITAR

...A NEW APPROACH TO ARPEGGIOS AND THEIR RELATIONSHIP TO CHORDS AND SCALES. FOR THE ROCK, BLUES, AND JAZZ GUITARIST.

by DON LATARSKI

INTRODUCTION

An arpeggio is a series of chord tones played one note at a time. Every serious guitarist must at some point master many of the primary arpeggio forms such as maj7th, min7th, aug7th, etc.

Arpeggios are frequently used in constructing melodies. A quick analysis of melodies from music of nearly all ages and styles will demonstrate this fact. They are also used as accompaniment devices.

In contemporary music, such as rock, blues and jazz, arpeggios are used as improvisational tools along with scales. It is for musicians who play in these styles that this book is intended.

In any given improvisational situation, the "safest" sounding pitch will always be a chord tone. However, if your solo is made up only of chord tones, you run the risk of boring your listeners. Good solos are made up of a variety of rhythmic, melodic and harmonic devices. It's up to each person to find the proper balance between playing it safe and taking chances.

Arpeggios are very useful in particular to the jazz musician because this style of music often requires the improvisor to make quick key shifts when soloing. Many guitarists use arpeggios to facilitate these kind of changes. The arpeggio has the benefit of outlining the harmony that's happening at the moment, letting the listener know that the improvisor has a firm grasp of the harmonic movement in the piece. Also, the use of arpeggios has the effect of breaking up the flow of the musical line by interspersing intervallic leaps into the solo. Solos made up of just scale passages tend to sound smooth and vocal-like. Wide interval leaps provide contrast in the line.

Learning arpeggios on the guitar is more than just learning chord forms. Chords are usually played one note per string. In some cases, it's possible to play one, two or three notes per string in an arpeggio. This will become very obvious once you get into the book.

The format of this book is simple. Each page contains a particular type of chord, which is shown in five different forms. The root of each chord form is shown as a solid black dot. The dot is your reference note. By using this note, you can move the chord form up and down the fingerboard to play this chord on any fret and in any key.

The middle column shows the arpeggio of the chord to its left. The right column shows the larger scale pattern which goes with this arpeggio and chord. You get the whole picture, from the chord to its arpeggio to the complete scale. An X above a string means you must either mute the string or strings or simply not pluck it if you are using your fingers.(Many of these chords will be easier to play if you pluck the strings with your fingers instead of trying to strum them with a pick.)

On some of the more complicated chords such as Dom9b5, I've shaded in some of the notes in an attempt to make things a little clearer as to what are important notes and what are not. In some cases, the root will be shaded, because the root is not really a necessary note in an arpeggio. For the most part, the chords are in root position, with the bass note being the lowest note of the chord. In some cases, this was not possible. At any rate, all chord voicings are shown. (These are the numbers inside the circles in each chord form.) Five different forms of each chord type are given. This approach effectively covers the entire length of the fingerboard.

The scales I chose to show with each chord type are what your "average" garden variety jazz musician might have chosen. However, don't be fooled into thinking that these are the only possibilities, because they aren't. I encourage you to seek out other books on the subject of improvisation or check out my book entitled, SCALE PATTERNS FOR GUITAR. Scale choice is dependant upon how any given chord is functioning in a song. A good jazz theory text and qualified instructor can put this subject in perspective for you.

It's up to you to choose what order to play the notes which make up any arpeggio. You don't have to start from the lowest note and go right up from there. You can start anywhere you like and play the notes in any order. Also, you'll have to work out your own fingerings for the chord forms, arpeggios and scales. The numbers which are included in each chord, scale and arpeggio, are the scale degrees you are playing. Eventually, you must know what you're doing when you are playing these things, so start now to know what's going on with your playing.

Practice these arpeggios by first hitting a chord, then the arpeggio which goes with it, and then the larger scale. This will take you across the page from left to right. You need to have the arpeggio in your fingers as fluently as the chords and scales. Think of the arpeggios as the bridge between chords and scales.

Most guitarists who've grown up playing rock and blues styles are often trapped by a mono-scalar approach to soloing. That is, they try to use one scale, usually the minor pentatonic or blues, as it's often called, to play over a series of changing chords. In many cases, this works well because what they call chords are really not. They are intervals of a perfect 5th, also known as power chords. This type of approach doesn't work to well when the harmony consists of moving triads and four note chords (7th's). This type of harmonic movement makes your scale seem inadequate and out of place. You need different tonal resources, i.e., new scales, to effectively solo over the changes. All guitarists run up against this problem sooner of later, especially if they want to move into songs which have a jazz leaning.

Two of the earliest jazz guitarists that relied heavily on arpeggios are Django Reinhardt and Charlie Christian. Listen to how they used arpeggios to follow the contour of the moving chord progressions. You'll soon see the art involved in this type of approach. For a more modern approach, listen to guitarists like Pat Metheny, John Scofield and Mike Stern.

Experimentation is the key to becoming an accomplished improvisor. There's no substitute. The things in this book are meant to get you started down this path. And if you find these arpeggios helpful, please check out my other books. In addition to the SCALE PATTERNS FOR GUITAR, mentioned earlier, I've also written: MOVEABLE GUITAR CHORDS, INTRODUCTION TO CHORD THEORY, CHORD EMBELLISH-MENT and CHORD ORBITS.

Don Latarski

About the author...

Don Latarski has been playing the guitar since 1963. He's an adjunct faculty member at the University of Oregon's Music School. In addition to this book, he's written a number of others on guitar instruction: *Introduction to Chord Theory, Moveable Guitar Chords, Scale Patterns for Guitar, Arpeggios for Guitar* and *Chord Embellishment.* Known nationally as a a gifted guitarist and composer; Don performs frequently with his group at Jazz Festivals and Clubs in the Pacific Northwest. His music can be heard on "HAVEN", Inner City Records and "LIFELINE", PAUSA Records. Originally a Michigan native, Don has made Eugene, Oregon his home since 1973 where he builds and rides recumbant bicycles when it's not raining.

TABLE OF CONTENTS

Chord Type: Major triad

Scale/Mode:

Chord Form ⟶ Arpeggio ⟶ Ionian

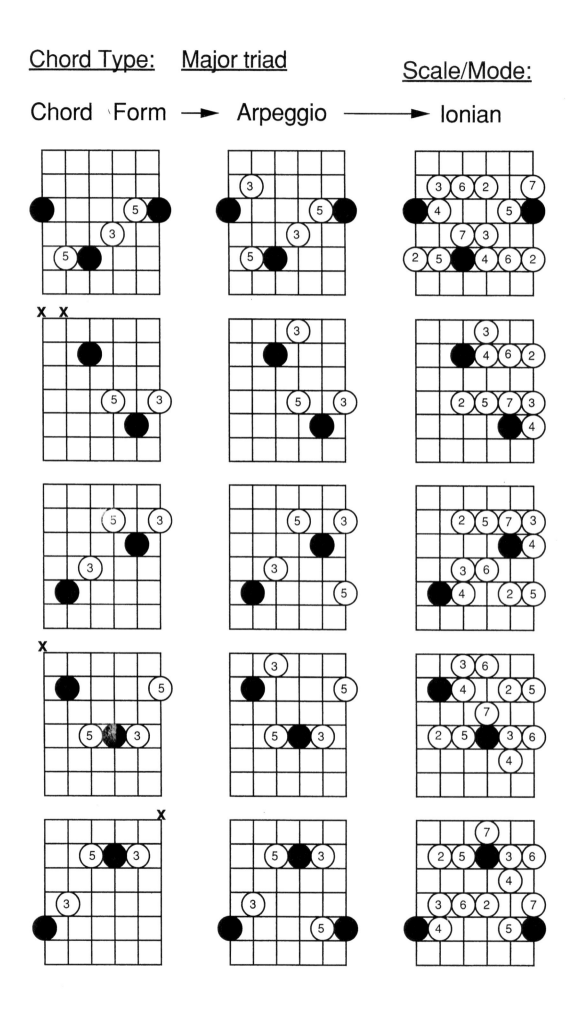

Chord Type: Major 6th   Scale/Mode :

Chord   Form → Arpeggio → Ionian

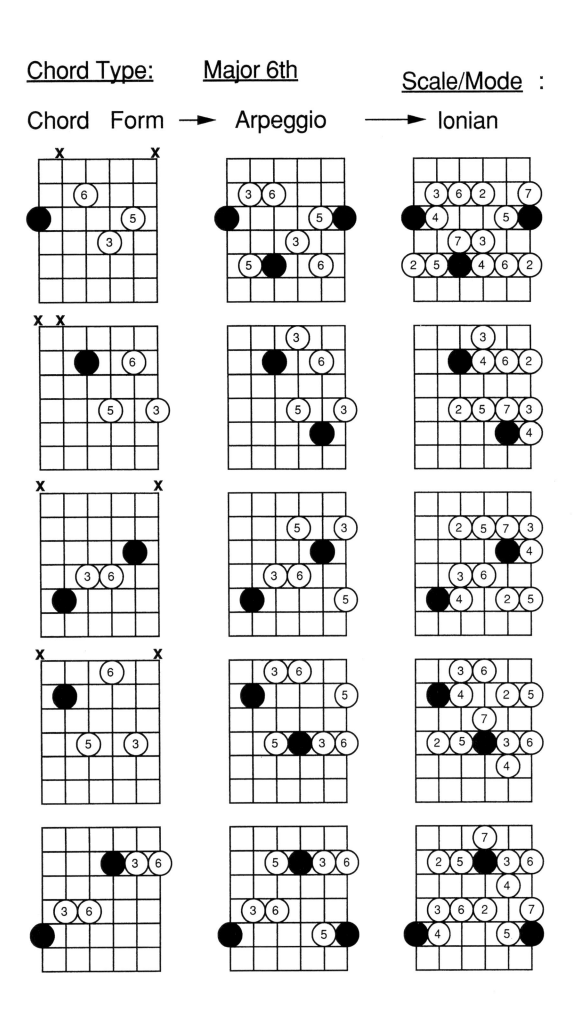

Chord Type: Major 7th

Scale/Mode:

Chord   Form ⟶ Arpeggio ⟶ Ionian

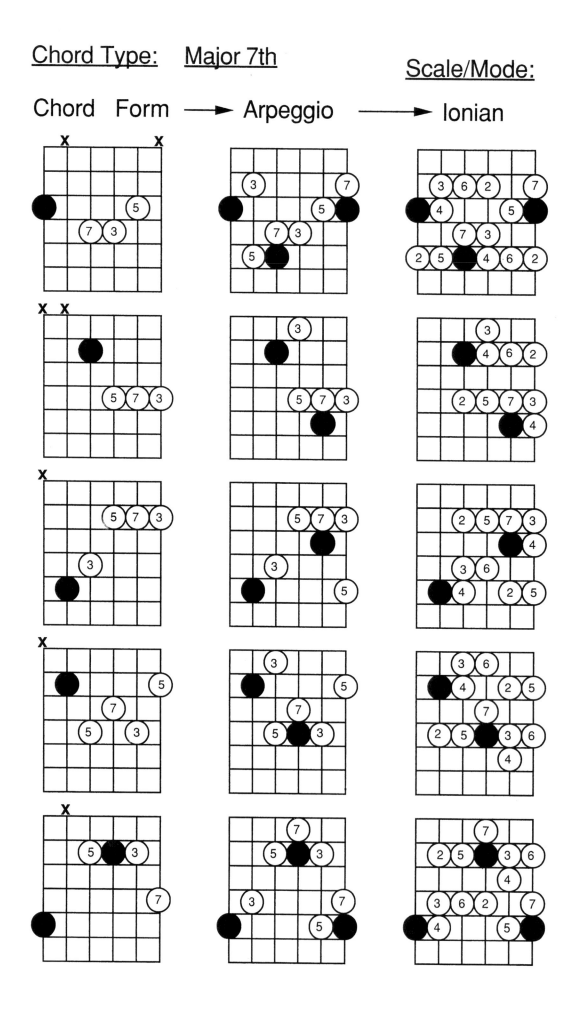

Chord Type: Major 6/9

Scale/Mode:

Chord Form ⟶ Arpeggio ⟶ Ionian

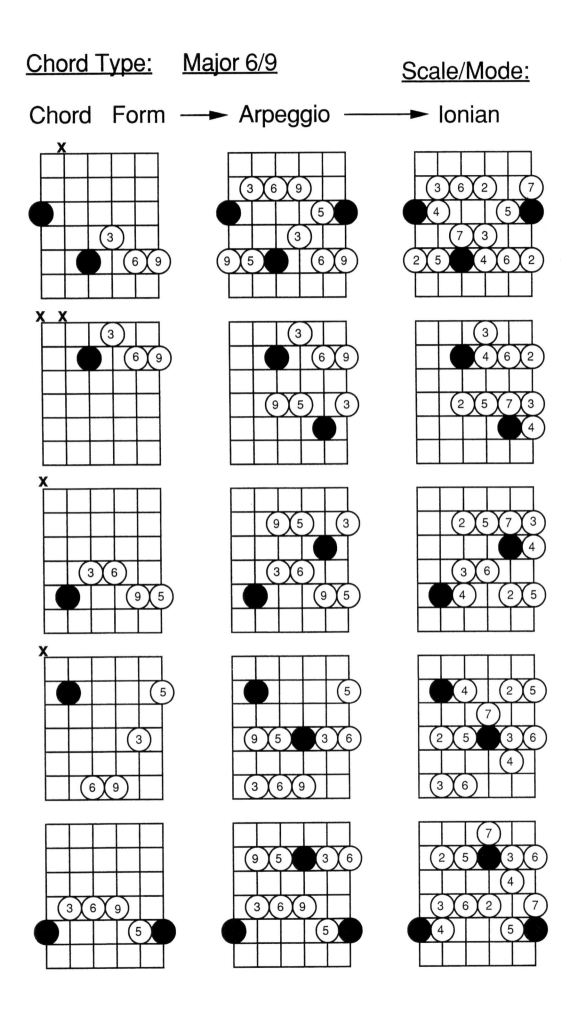

Chord Type: Major 7b5   Scale/Mode

Chord   Form   ⟶   Arpeggio   ⟶   Lydian

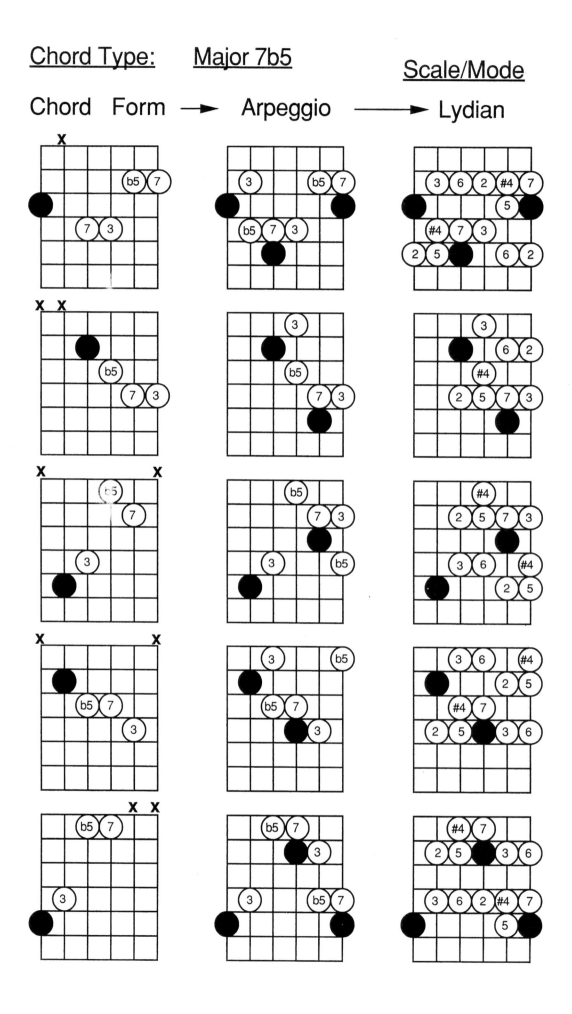

Chord Type: Major 7#5

Scale/Mode:

Chord Form ⟶ Arpeggio ⟶ Lydian-aug

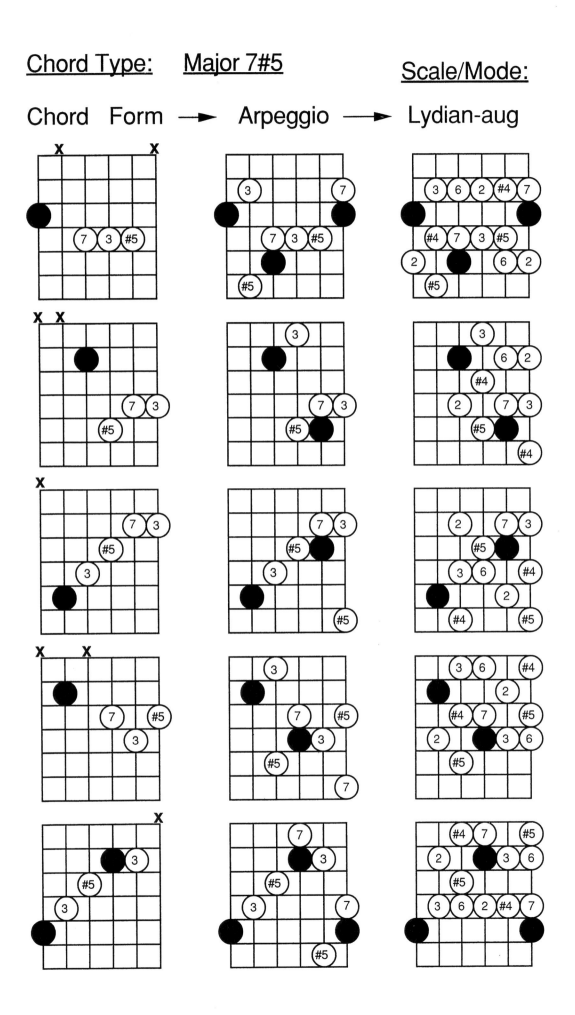

Chord Type: Major add 9

Scale/Mode:

Chord   Form → Arpeggio → Ionian

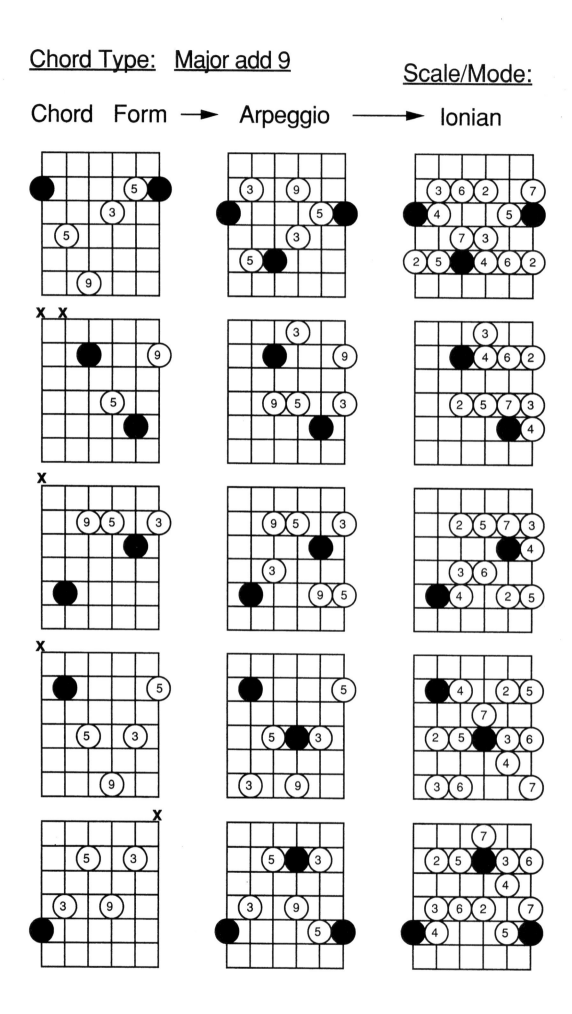

Chord Type: Major 9th   Scale/Mode:

Chord   Form ⟶ Arpeggio ⟶ Ionian

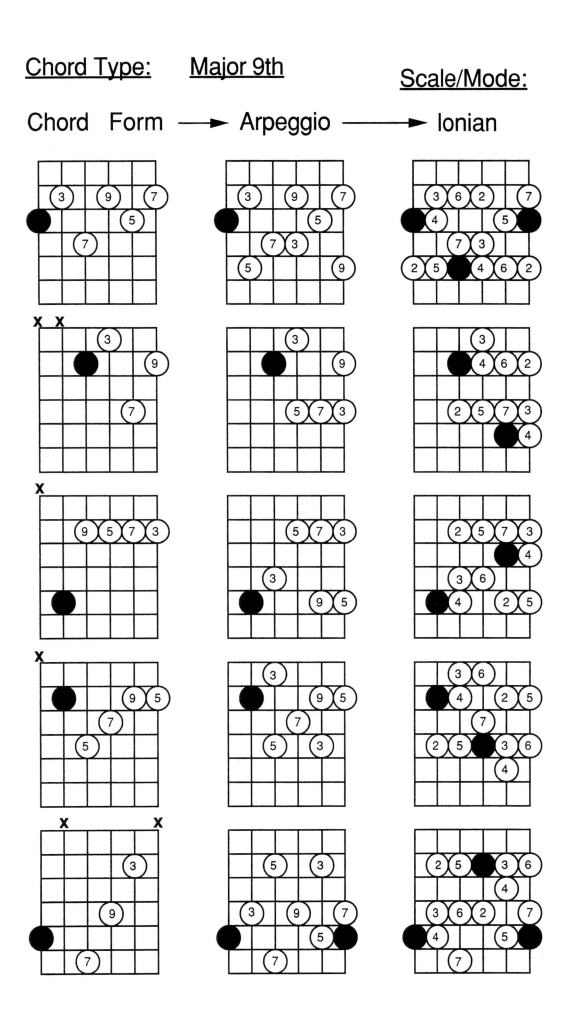

Chord Type: Minor triad

Scale/Mode:

Chord Form → Arpeggio → Dorian

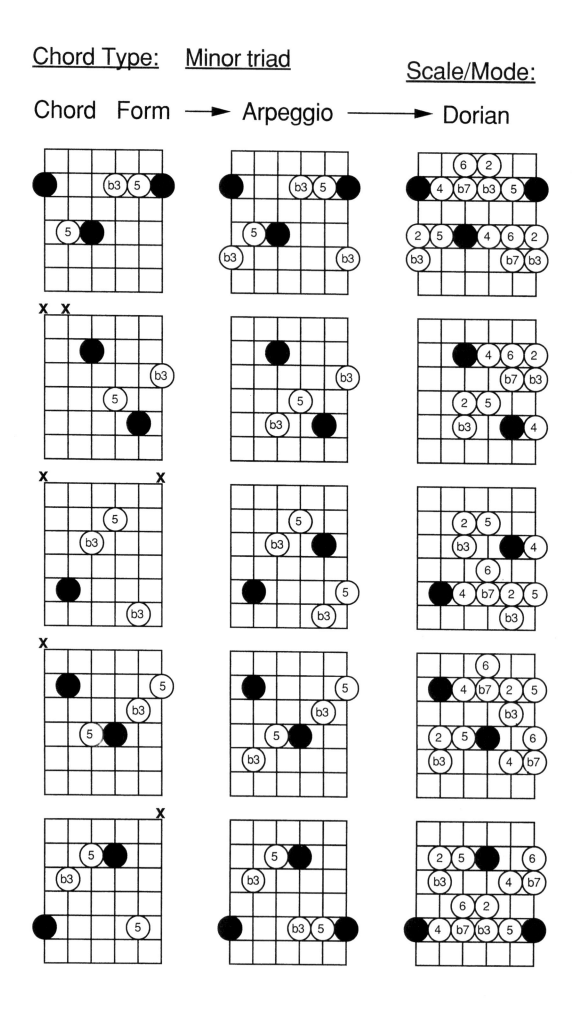

Chord Type: Minor 6th

Chord   Form ⟶ Arpeggio ⟶ Dorian

Scale/Mode:

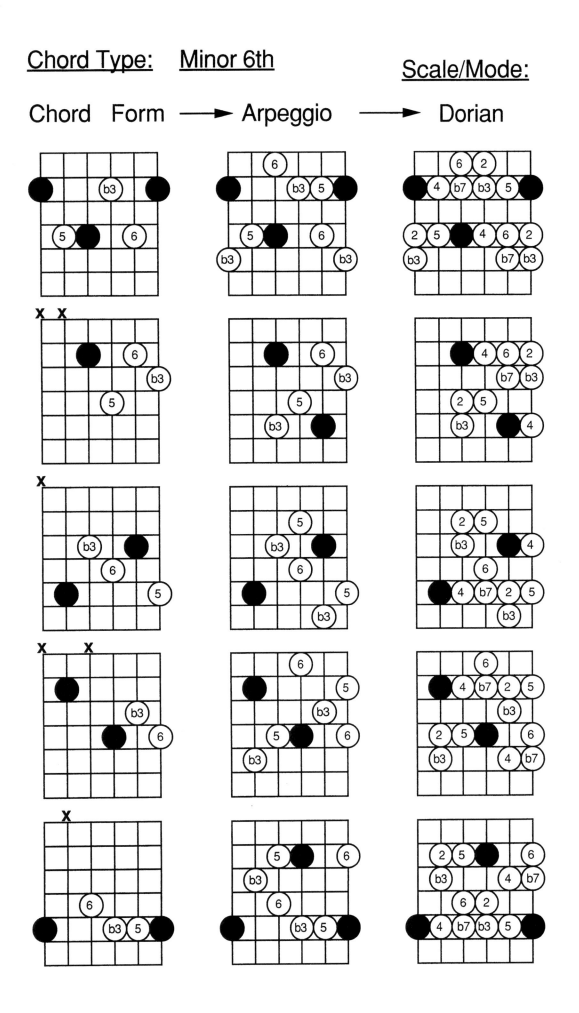

Chord Type: Minor 6/9

Scale/Mode:

Chord Form ⟶ Arpeggio ⟶ Dorian

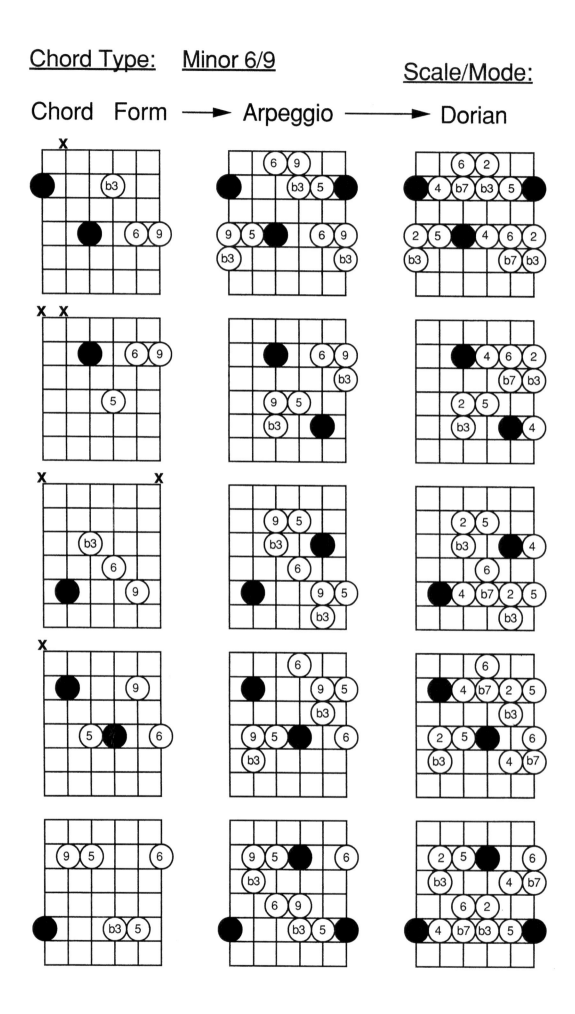

21

Chord Type: Minor 7th

Scale/Mode:

Chord Form ⟶ Arpeggio ⟶ Dorian

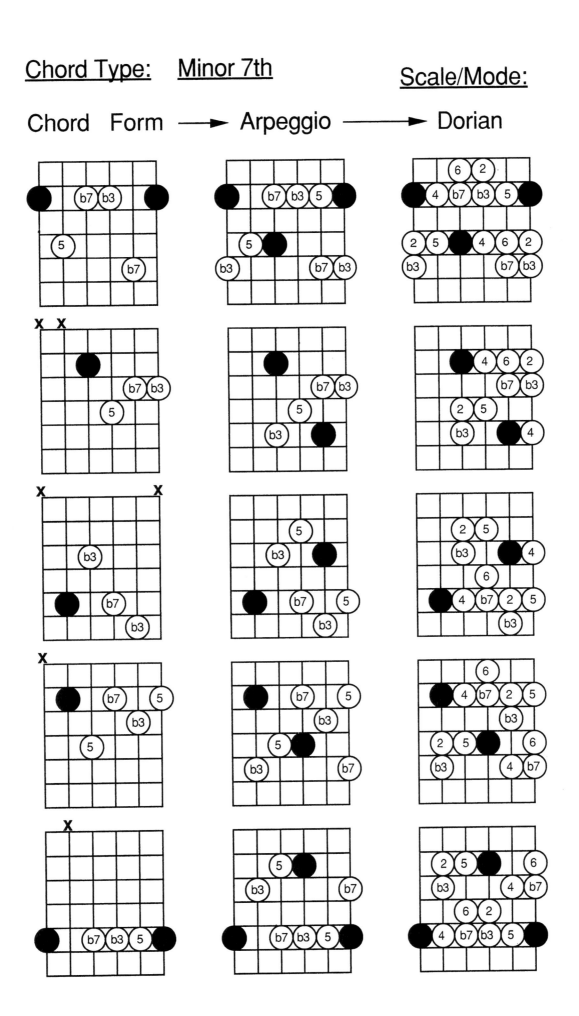

Chord Type: Minor #7th

Scale/Mode:

Chord   Form ⟶ Arpeggio ⟶ Melodic Min.

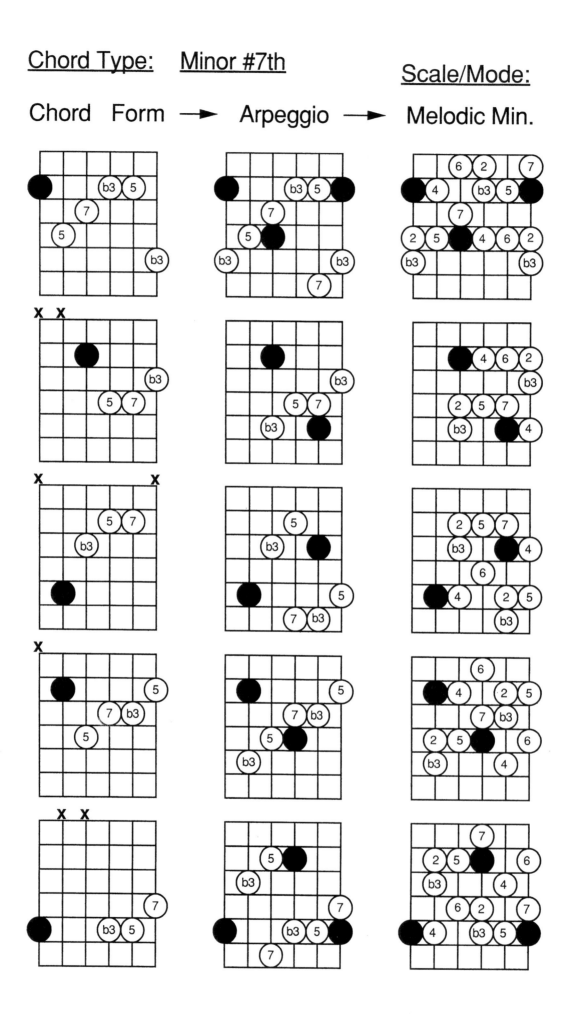

Chord Type: Minor 7b5   Scale/Mode:

Chord   Form ——→ Arpeggio ——→ Locrian

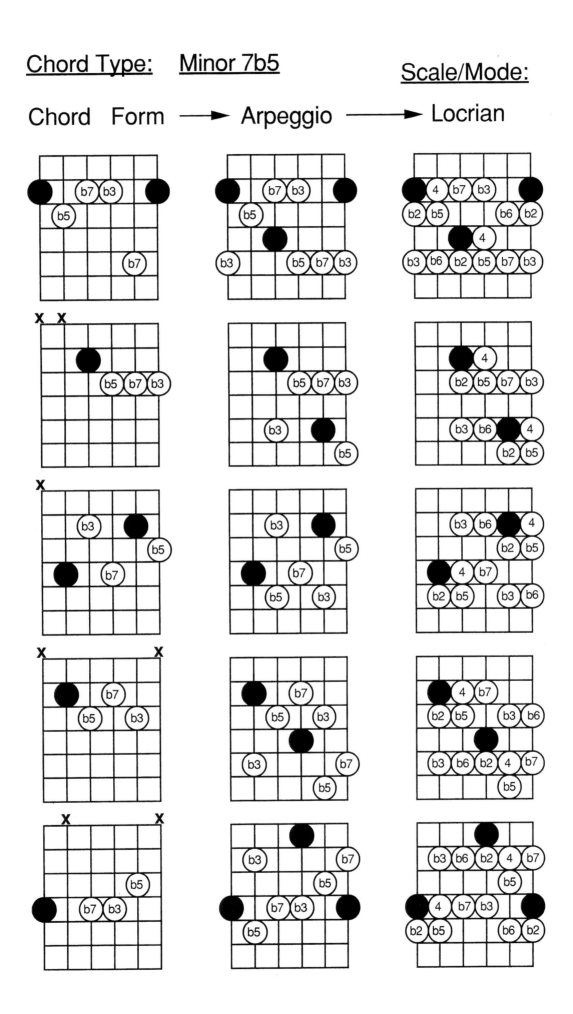

Chord Type: Minor add9 Scale/Mode:

Chord   Form ⟶ Arpeggio ⟶ Dorian

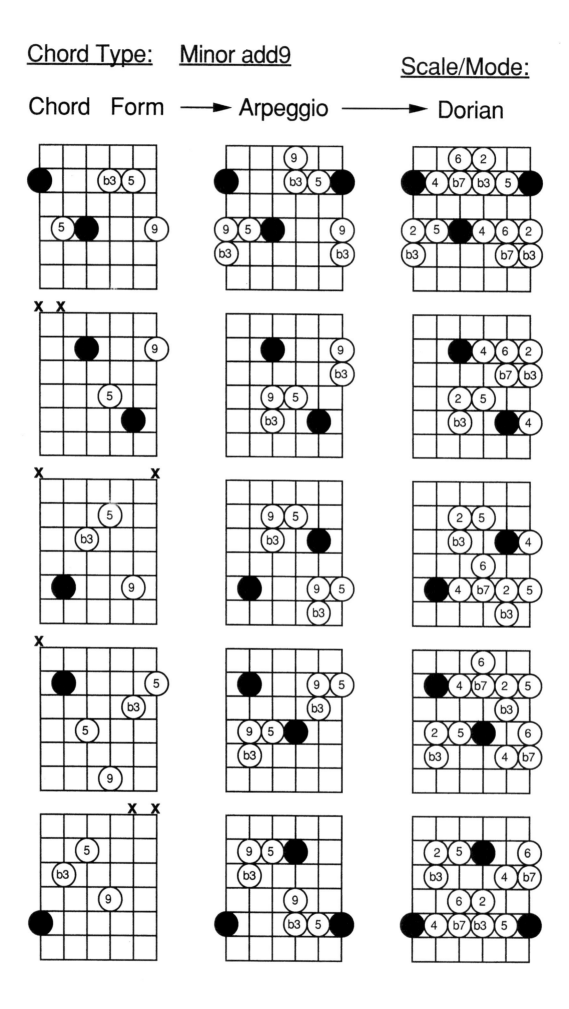

Chord Type: Minor 9th

Chord Form ⟶ Arpeggio ⟶ Dorian

Scale/Mode:

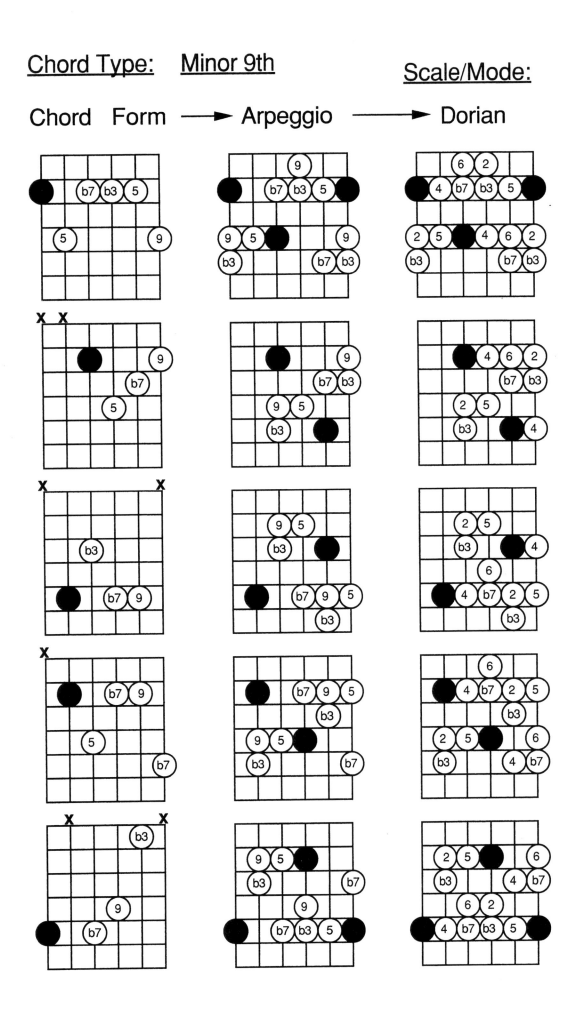

Chord Type: Minor 11th   Scale/Mode:

Chord   Form ⟶   Arpeggio ⟶ Dorian

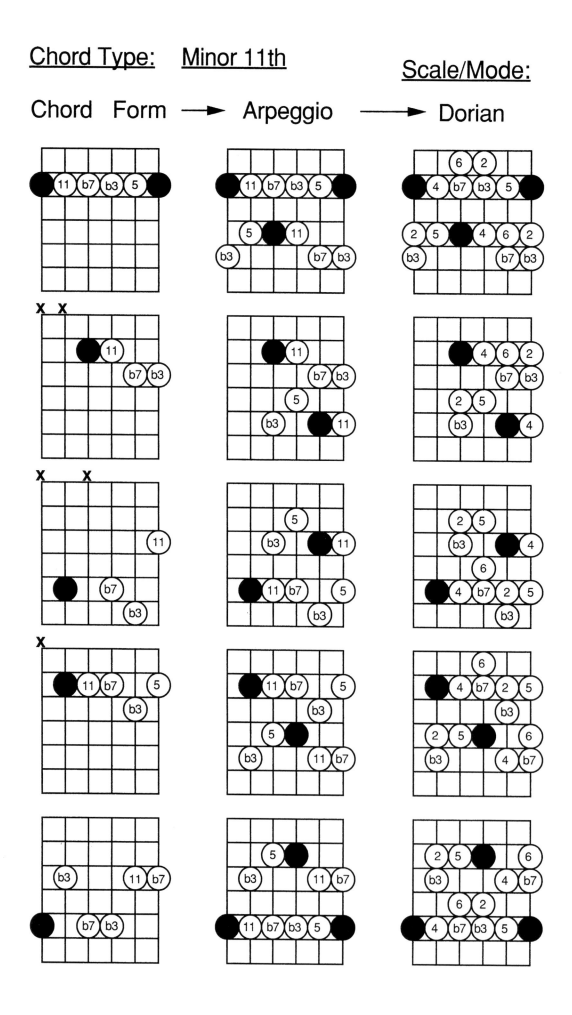

Chord Type: Dominant 7th

Scale/Mode:

Chord Form → Arpeggio → Mixolydian

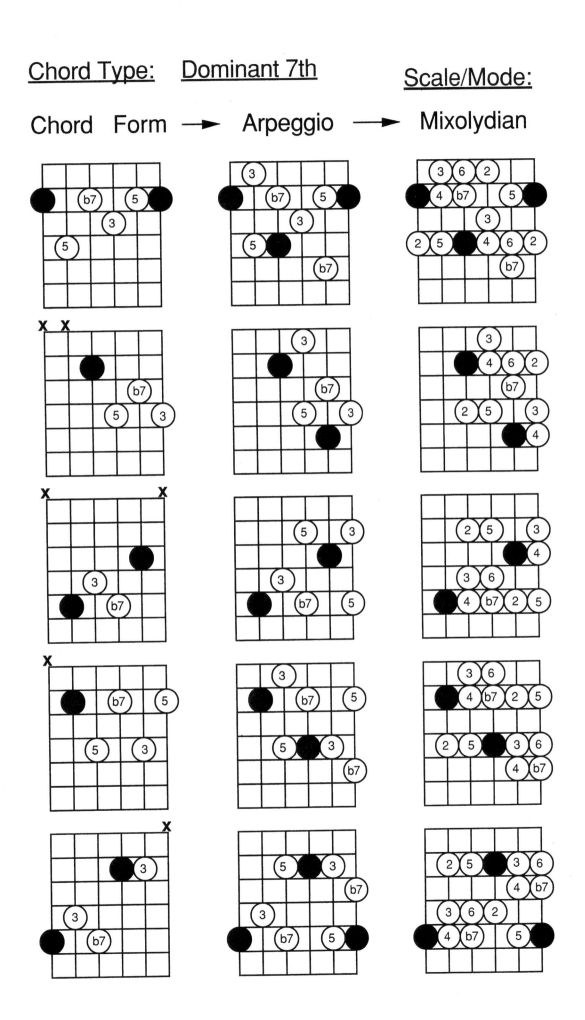

Chord Type: Dominant 7#11   Scale/Mode:

Chord   Form →   Arpeggio →   Super Locrian

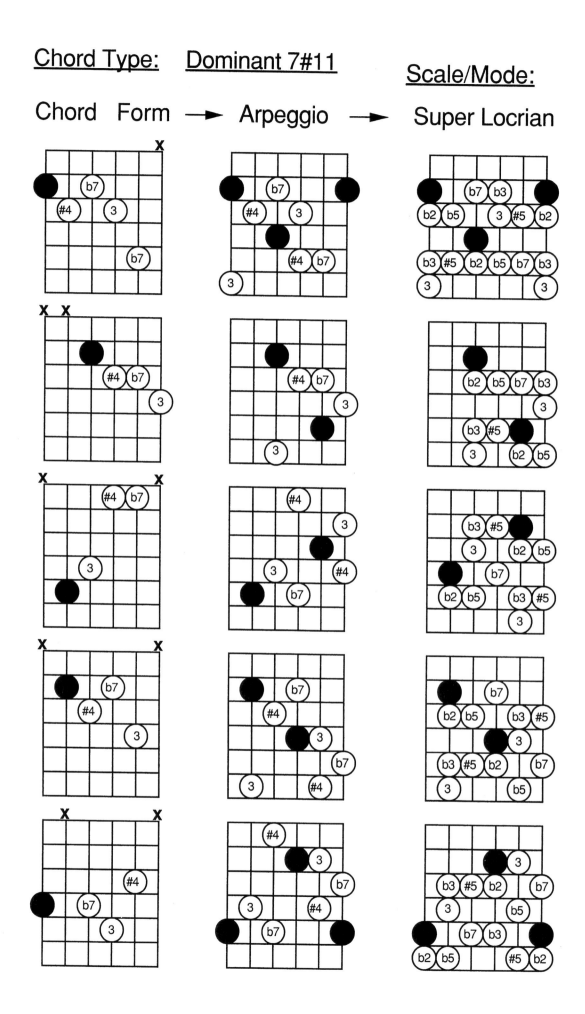

Chord Type: Dominant 7b9

Scale/Mode:

Chord Form ➔ Arpeggio ➔ Diminished h/w

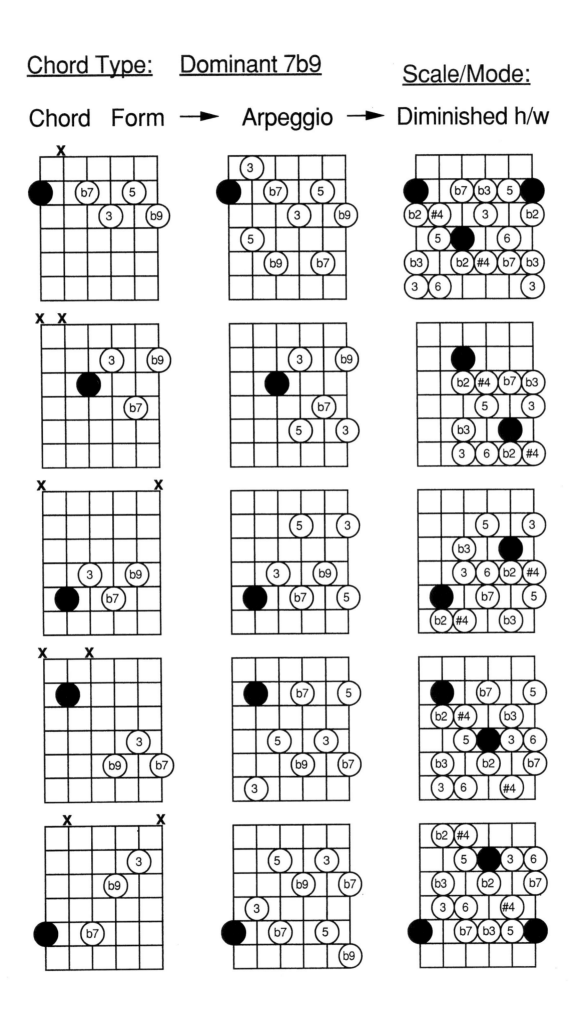

30

Chord Type: Dominant 7#9   Scale/Mode:

Chord Form → Arpeggio → Blues

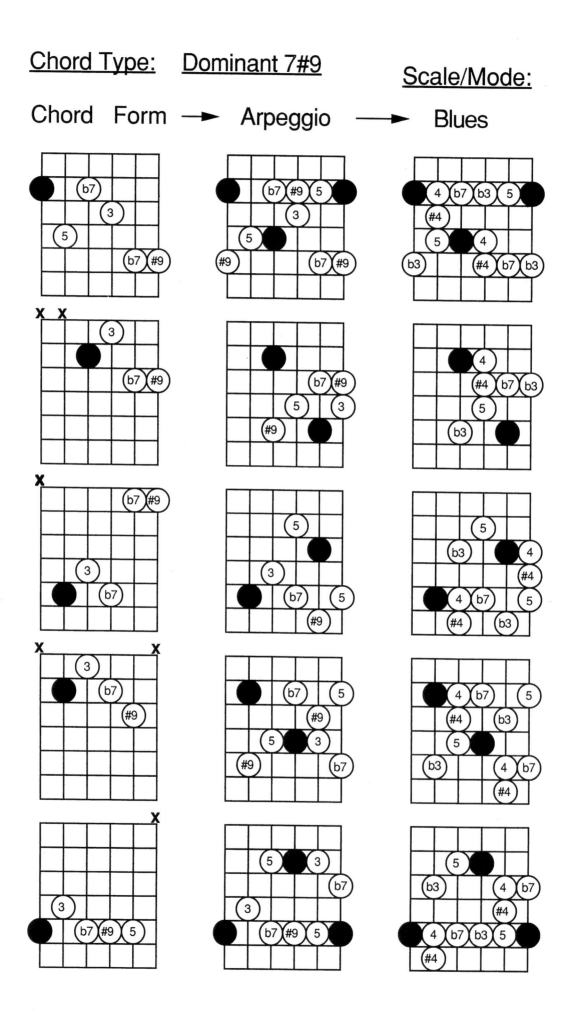

Chord Type: Dominant 7b5b9   Scale/Mode:

Chord   Form →   Arpeggio →   Super Locrian

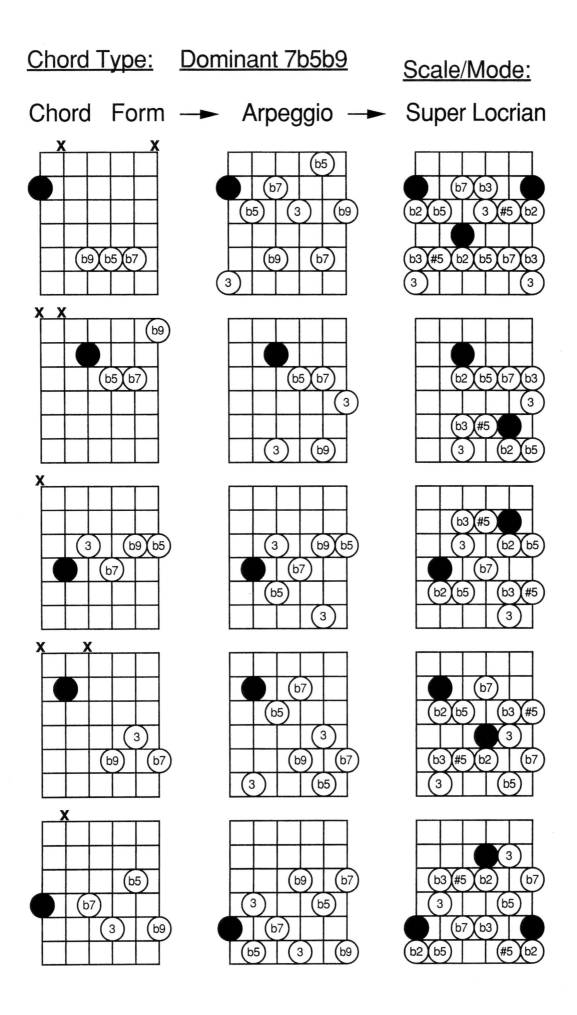

Chord Type: Dominant 7#5#9

Scale/Mode:

Chord Form → Arpeggio → Super Locrian

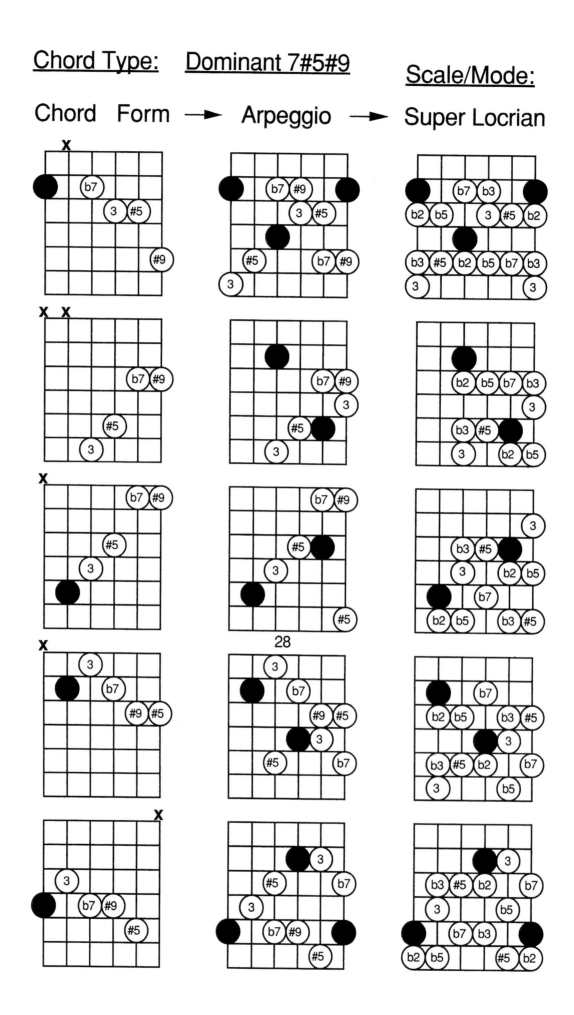

Chord Type: Dominant 7#5b9   Scale/Mode:

Chord Form → Arpeggio → Super Locrian

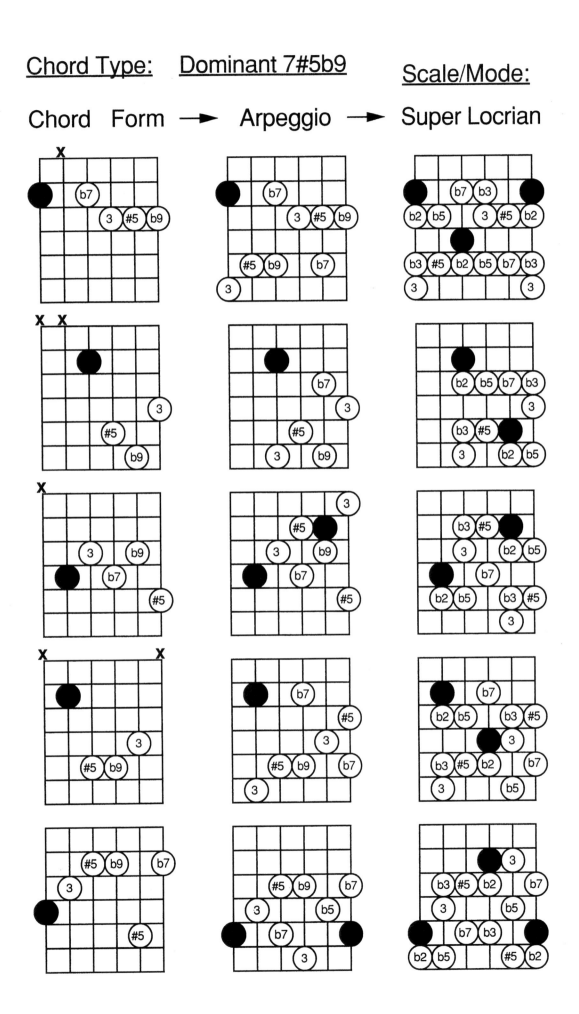

Chord Type: Dominant 7b5#9

Chord Form → Arpeggio → ## Scale/Mode: Super Locrian

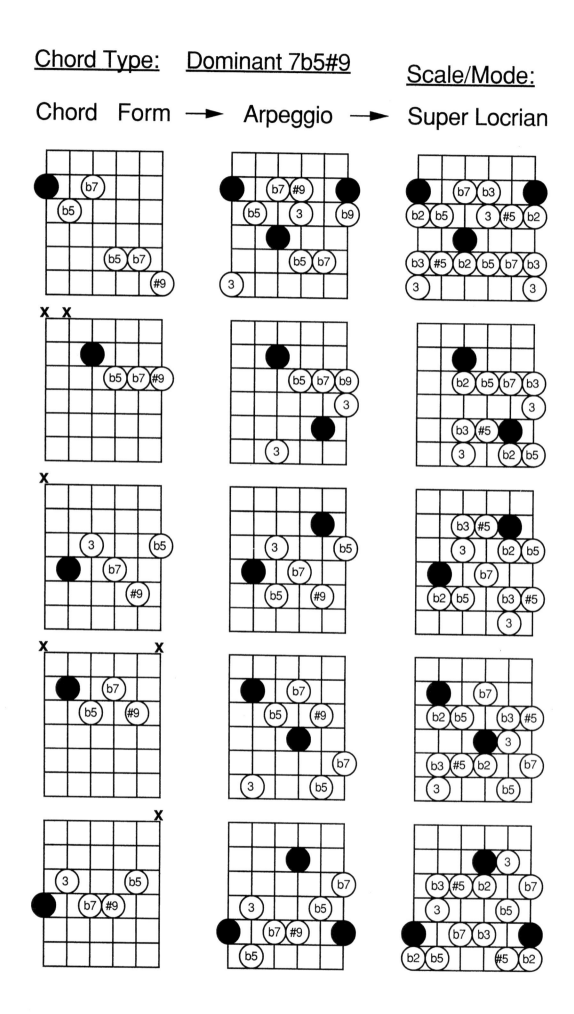

Chord Type: Dominant 9th   Scale/Mode:

Chord   Form → Arpeggio → Mixolydian

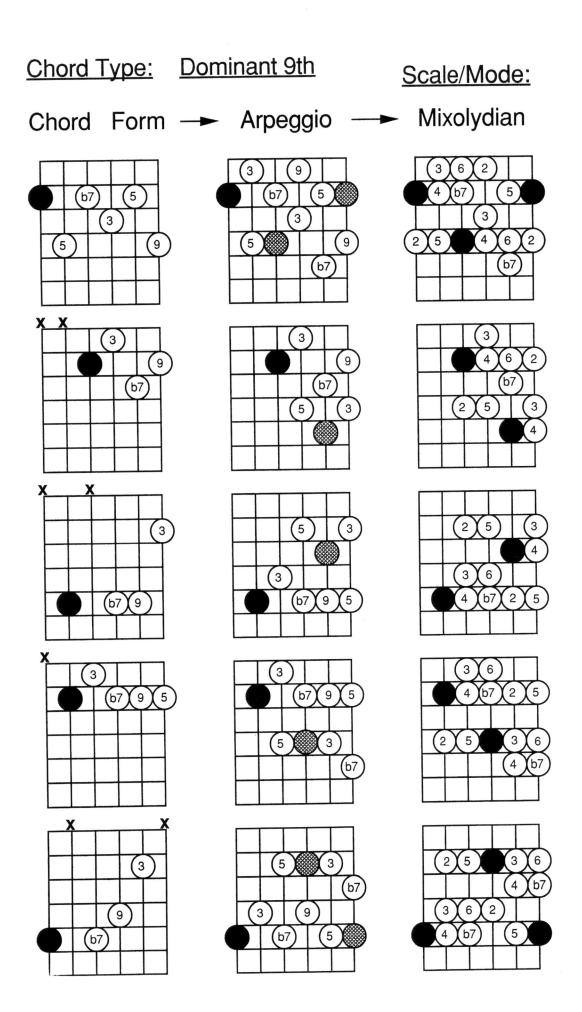

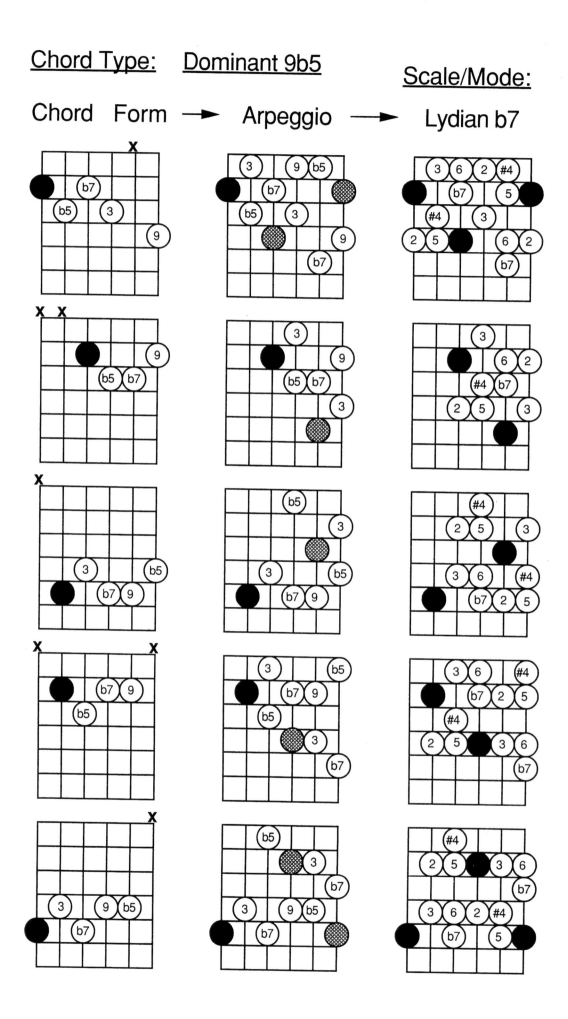

Chord Type: Dominant 9b5

Chord   Form → Arpeggio → Lydian b7

Scale/Mode:

Chord Type: Dominant 9#5   Scale/Mode:

Chord Form → Arpeggio → Mixolydian b6

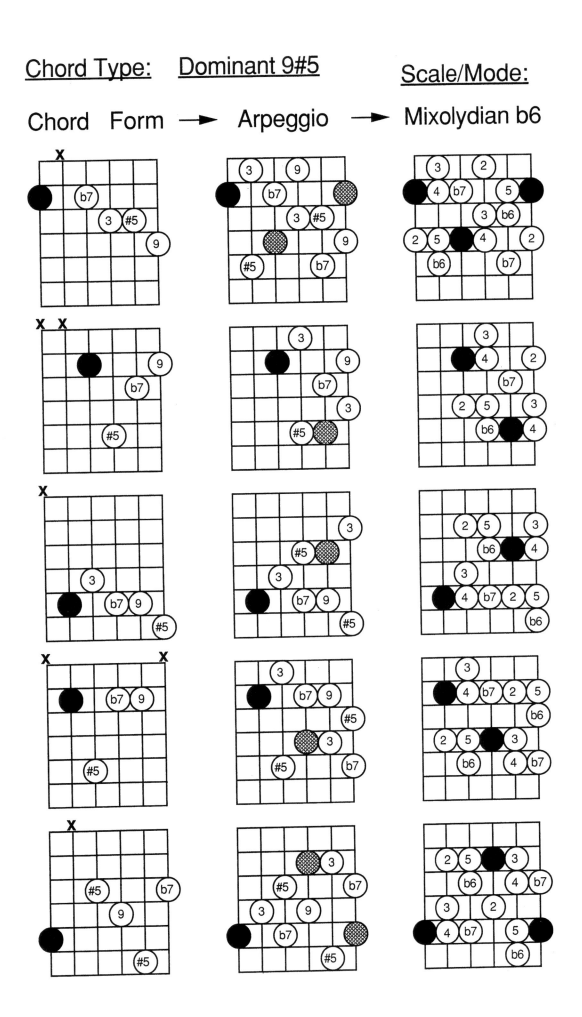

Chord Type: Dominant 13th

Chord Form → Arpeggio → Scale/Mode: Mixolydian

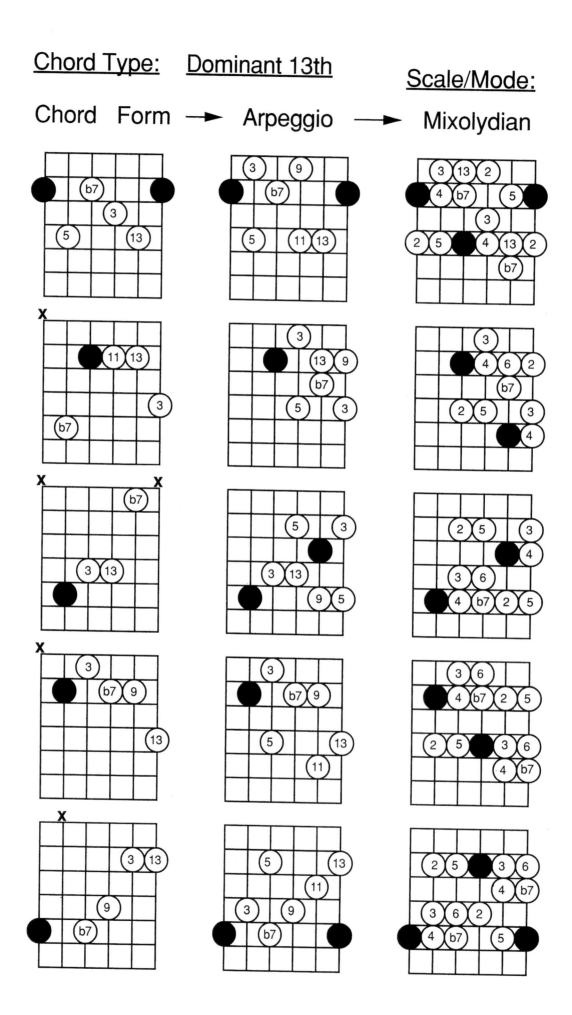

Chord Type: Dominant 13b5   Scale/Mode:

Chord Form ⟶ Arpeggio ⟶ Lydian b7

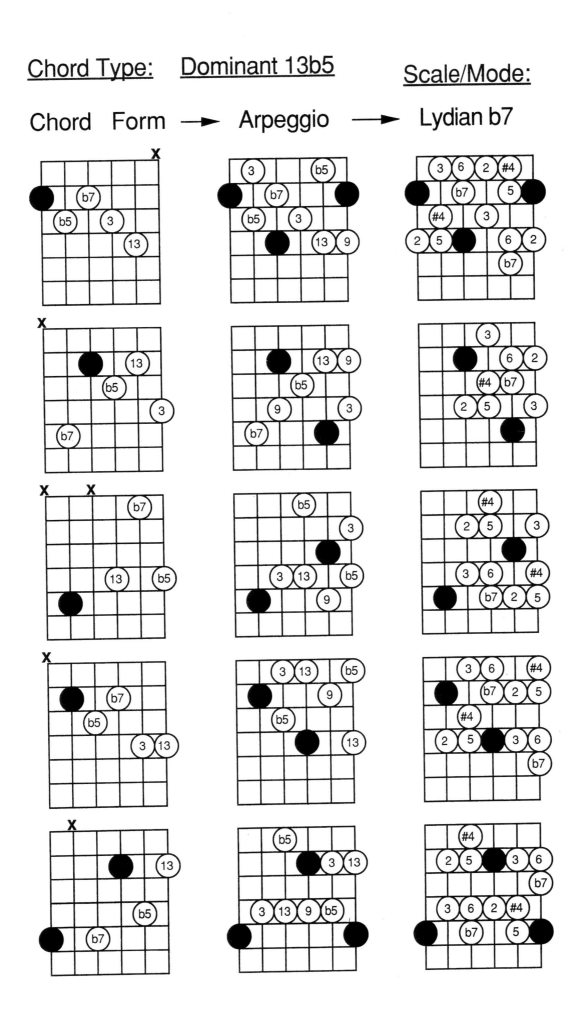

Chord Type: Dominant 13b9

Chord Form → Arpeggio → Scale/Mode: Diminished h/w

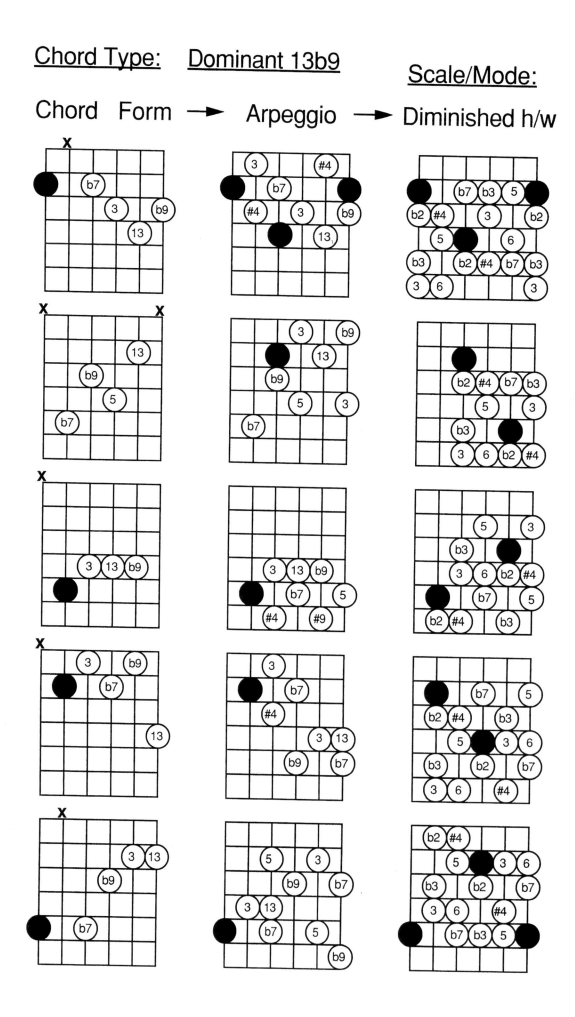

Chord Type: Dominant 13#9

Chord   Form →   Arpeggio →   Scale/Mode:

Diminished h/w

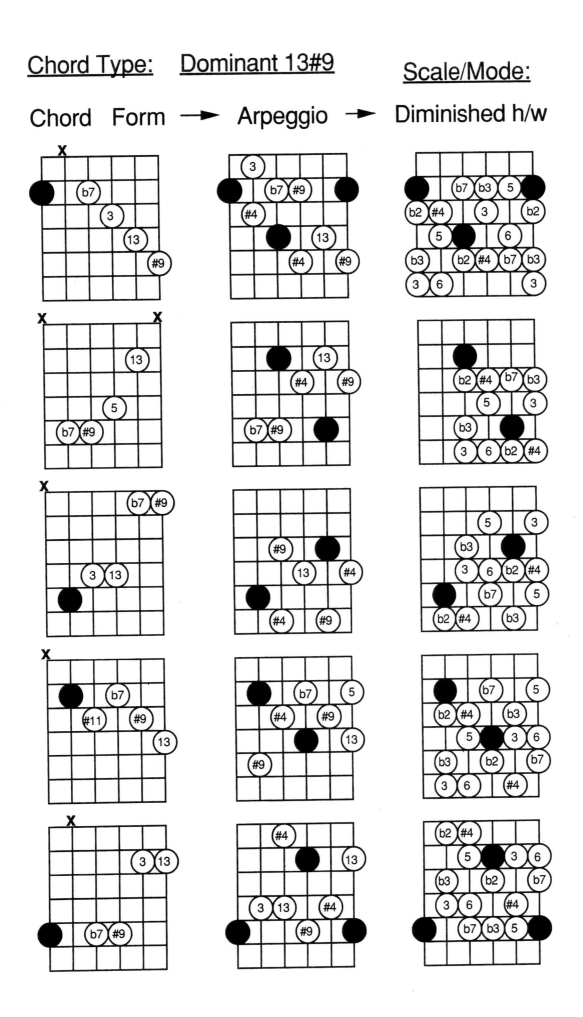

Chord Type: Suspended 7th

Scale/Mode:

Chord Form → Arpeggio → Mixolydian

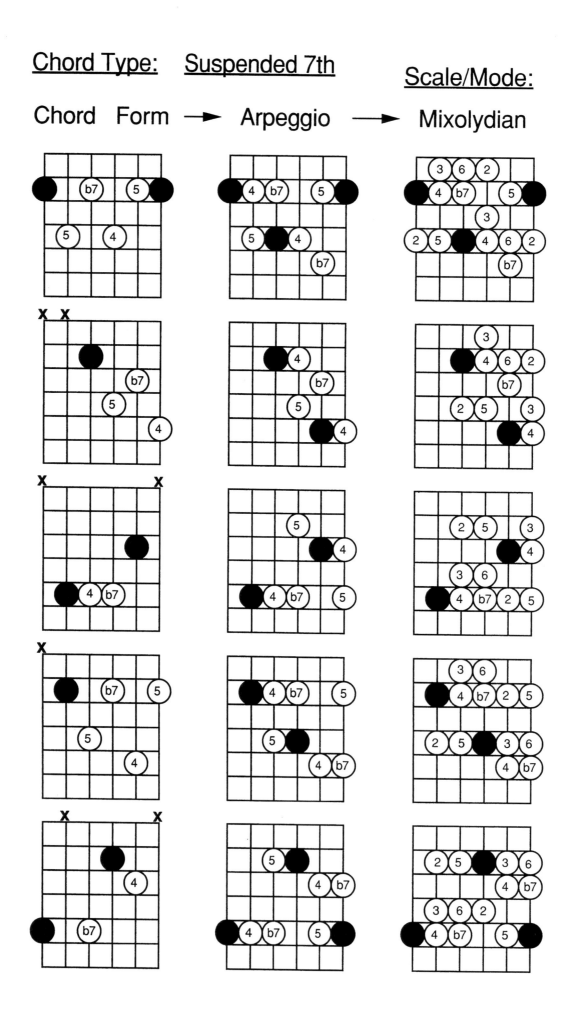

43

Chord Type: <u>Suspended 9th</u>

Scale/Mode:

Chord Form → Arpeggio → Mixolydian

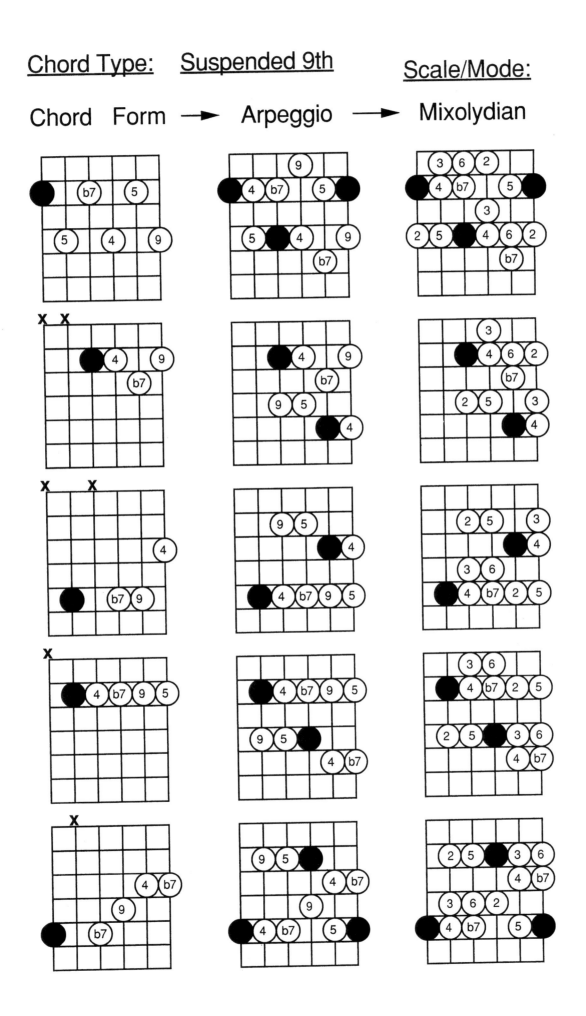

Chord Type: Augmented Triad   Scale/Mode:

Chord   Form →   Arpeggio →   Whole Tone

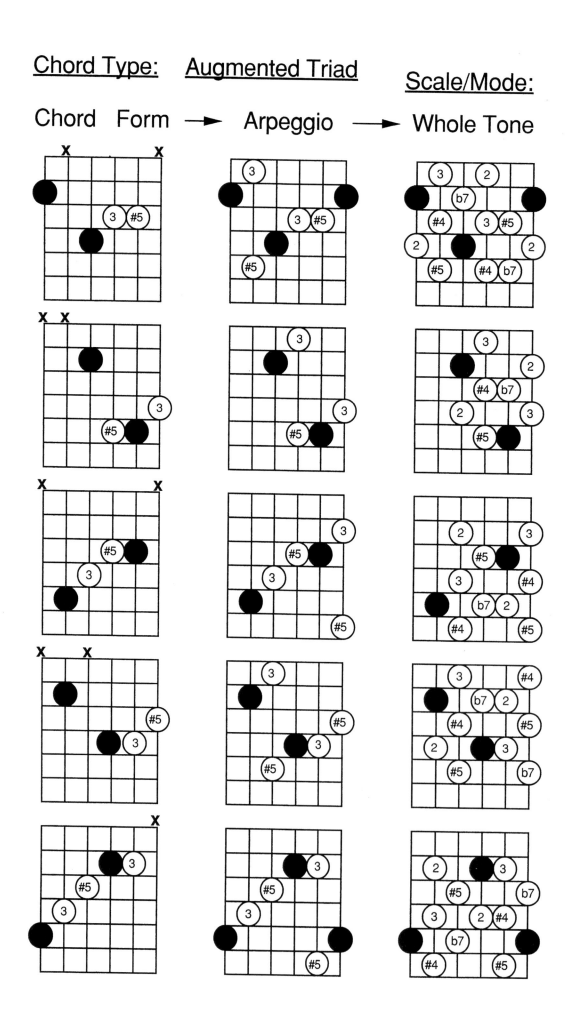

Chord Type: Augmented 7th   Scale/Mode:

Chord Form ⟶ Arpeggio ⟶ Whole Tone

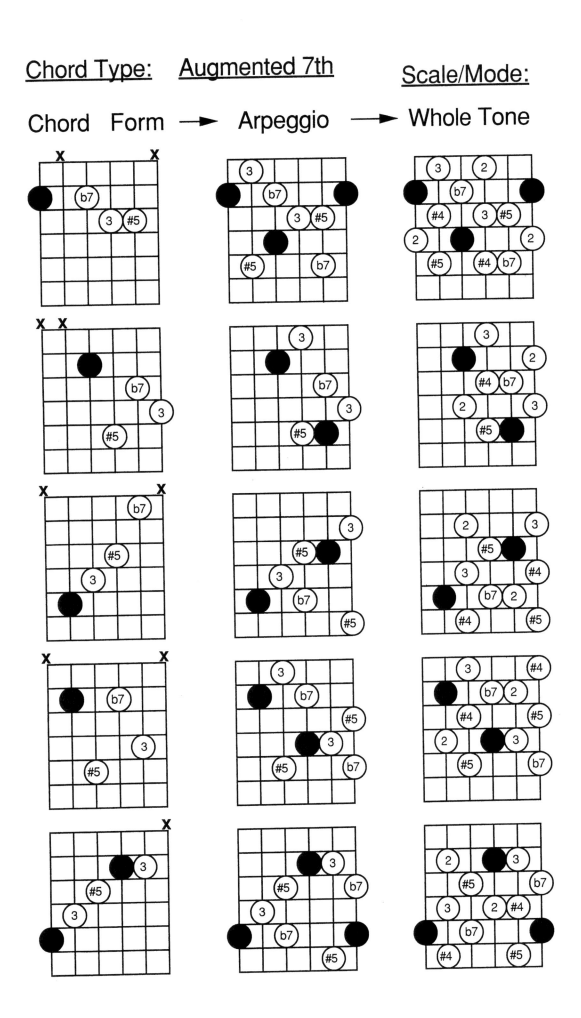

Chord Type: Diminished 7th

Scale/Mode:

Chord   Form → Arpeggio → Diminished w/h

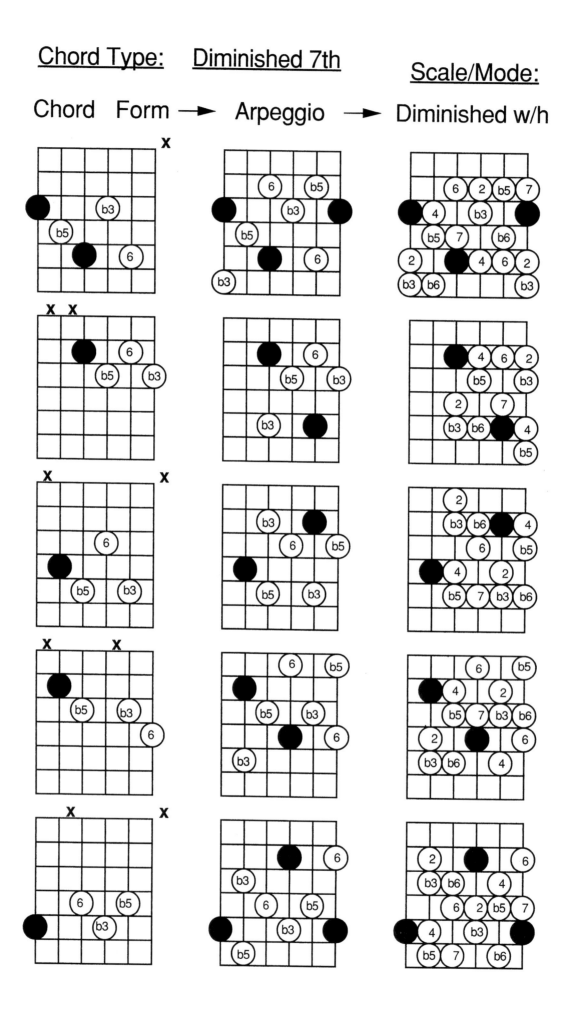